I Feel Like a Giant!

9 Steps To Building Confidence

By
Ryan and Elizabeth Stream

Building confidence is a process that takes time and effort, but it is a worthwhile investment in oneself. By implementing these 9 steps into your daily life, you can begin to build confidence and become the best version of yourself.

Remember that building confidence is a journey, and it's important to celebrate your progress along the way. With dedication and perseverance, you can achieve your goals and overcome any obstacles that may come your way!

Ryan and Elizabeth Stream

Greetings everyone! My name is Ryan Stream, and I am honored to introduce myself and my wife, Elizabeth, as your guides on this journey through our book on building more confidence. As a motivational speaker, award-winning musician, best-selling author, two-time military veteran, and entrepreneur, I have had the privilege of pursuing many passions and achieving great success in my life. It is my pleasure to share some tips on a few things that have helped me achieve this success.

I am grateful that you have chosen to join us on this journey to develop greater confidence, and I also want to express my appreciation to those of you who have read my previous book, "Conquering Your Colosseum."

In "Conquering Your Colosseum," I shared five principles that have helped me build an extraordinary life filled with purpose, passion, and joy. These principles are based on my personal experiences and insights, and I believe they can be applied by anyone (like you!) who seeks to create a fulfilling life for themselves. My aim with both my previous book and this one is to provide *actionable* and *relatable* advice that can help you overcome your fears, doubts, and limitations and become the best version of yourself. And maybe, just maybe, you will (as I have at times), feel like a giant as you achieve your goals and start living the life you have dreamed of. Are you excited?

Let me introduce my wife Elizabeth, who is a truly remarkable individual who has worn many hats in her life. From her successful lifestyle blog to her modeling career, her business savvy, and her passion for helping others, Elizabeth has proved time and time again that she is a force to be reckoned with! Elizabeth has overcome numerous challenges in her life, including the difficult experience of giving birth to her first child while her husband was away fighting in Afghanistan. After her husband returned home, their family faced additional struggles, which Elizabeth worked hard to overcome.

As a Hispanic student who arrived in America not knowing English, Elizabeth initially struggled to navigate the American classroom. However, she refused to let this setback hold her back and instead used it as motivation to succeed. Today, Elizabeth is a successful business owner and investor who is passionate about helping others feel confident and beautiful. Her commitment to this goal is evident in her laser teeth whitening business, Stream Beauty, where Elizabeth's clients leave her studio with bright, shining smiles that they can't wait to show off.

"We have learned so much throughout our lives and still have so much to learn. However, one thing we enjoy working on is our confidence."

Table of Contents

Chapter 1: Choice 1

Chapter 2: One of a Kind 15

Chapter 3: Nutritious Eating and Exercising 33

Chapter 4: Fail Forward - Be Brave Enough to Fail 43

Chapter 5: Identify 60

Chapter 6: Dedication 73

Chapter7: Education 83

Chapter 8: Navigate 89

Chapter 9: Truth 97

Chapter 1

Choice

In the first chapter of my book, "Conquering Your Colosseum," I recount the story of a difficult time in my past. My brothers and I were spending some nights in a homeless shelter and different foster homes. One by one, we were separated from each other, feeling lost, alone, and scared. After two years, thankfully all of us were reunited and adopted by the same family. However, all throughout my childhood I struggled and hid my true feelings. How? Behind my loud mouth and outgoing personality! Although I was too young to fully comprehend the concept of confidence, I found myself drawn to characters like the Power Rangers and Ninja Turtles who exuded bravery and fearlessness in the face of danger. While I didn't fully understand what gave them the strength to fight the bad guys, I admired their courage and wished I could be just like them.

In my teenage years, my biological mother passed away after losing her battle with depression. As I stood by my mother's casket, I felt an overwhelming sense of confusion and loss. It was hard to fathom that the person who brought me into this world was no longer with us. As I grappled with my emotions,

Choice

my brother placed a belated birthday gift in the casket. I couldn't help but wonder if giving her the gift on time would have made a difference, whether she would have felt loved enough to stay. I couldn't comprehend how someone could feel so hopeless that they could choose to end their own life.

As a teenager, I lacked comprehension of the weight that our choices and decisions hold, that decisions impact not only ourselves but also those around us. After walking away from my mother's casket, the next eight years of my life were filled with a series of law-breaking, lawsuits, and homelessness, all stemming from my own poor choices. The weight of my court fines amounted to over $30,000, a daunting financial burden at a young age.

In an effort to escape my challenging circumstances, I chose to join the military and even took steps to serve in Afghanistan, which helped me gain a little more confidence.

Shortly before deploying, I had the fortunate encounter of meeting Elizabeth, who would later become my wife and co-author of this book. As a man, I remember the rush of emotions that coursed through me upon seeing her for the first time. Her perfect smile and dark hair had me grinning from ear to ear! At the time, however, I was still struggling with personal issues and addiction, and my lack of confidence left me feeling inadequate and unworthy of her love.

After countless court appearances and assessments from both judges and military leaders, I was finally deemed fit for duty

I Feel Like a Giant!

and given the green light to serve. At the time, though, I was young and naive, and I couldn't fully grasp the implications of my decision to go to war. Little did I know that the experiences I would face would be traumatic and life-changing, with both positive and negative effects on my personal life and relationships, including my marriage. It was a decision that would shape my future in ways I never could have imagined.

The first time I was deployed, was to Afghanistan, and our unit had an incredibly difficult mission. We were tasked with locating and clearing bombs that the Taliban had placed in routes used by US military convoys. During this first deployment, around 23 out of the 32 soldiers in my platoon had their vehicles blown up by IEDs, and tragically, one father and husband in my unit were killed.

Despite these challenges, upon returning home from war, I had the confidence to propose to Elizabeth. Nothing could stop me there! Two months after our wedding, I left for another tour in Afghanistan. During my second deployment to Afghanistan, my wife and I had to maintain our relationship online through the use of the technology available in 2012. Thankfully, I was able to witness the birth of our daughter, Nixeon. Upon my return home at 23 years old, I was overjoyed to finally embrace my wife and see our little girl for the first time at eight months old.! It was a beautiful moment, one that brought tears to our eyes. Despite the hardships I faced in my life over the years, such as hunger, homelessness, drug addiction, and struggles with mental health (because of my life before and after adoption), I never imagined I would experience a moment that would make me feel like a true champion.

But after arriving home after that second deployment, when I held my wife in my arms and met my newborn daughter for the first time, I felt invincible, and just like the superheroes I admired as a child. A giant, who could do anything!

But as time passed and I faced the harsh realities of everyday life that we all often face, such as searching for employment, marital issues, and job loss, my confidence slowly began to wane. But I look back on my childhood and teenage years and see that while I was always able to make choices that determined the direction of my life, both good and bad decisions taught me valuable lessons, and have truly made me into the man I am today. I wonder, what choices have you made that have led you to where you are today?

And it's not just the choices you have made that impact your life, future and general confidence to face the world. Our confidence is shaped by a multitude of factors, including the choices and decisions made by our parents. As children, we look to our parents for guidance and support, and their actions and words can either uplift or diminish our self-esteem. If our parents provide a nurturing and encouraging environment as we grow up, we are more likely to feel confident in ourselves and our abilities. Conversely, if they are overly critical or neglectful, our confidence may suffer.

As we grow older, our own choices and actions also play a significant role in shaping our confidence as they did mine. Positive experiences, such as achieving goals or receiving recognition for our accomplishments, can boost our self-esteem and make us feel more confident. On the other hand, making mistakes or facing setbacks can make us doubt ourselves and erode our confidence.

Therefore, it is important to recognize that both our parents' choices and our own choices can have a profound effect on our confidence throughout our lives. By surrounding ourselves with positive influences and making positive choices throughout our lives, we can cultivate and maintain a healthy level of self-confidence.

Life through Elizabeth's eyes:

I was born in Los Angeles in 1989, just like Ryan. My parents, who came to the United States from Mexico, were incredibly loving, hardworking, and determined to provide my brothers and me with a better life than they had. They sacrificed so much to make this possible, and it was in California that my mother gave birth to me. After living in LA, my parents moved back to Mexico, and my dad traveled all over playing as a drummer in a band. I have vivid memories of hearing my dad's music on the radio and watching him perform in front of large crowds of thousands of people.

Choice

While my dad was making music, my mother stayed at home and taught us how to be responsible children. Despite hearing my dad's band on the radio, we were not a well-off family. Like many musicians, my dad earned little money, and many people took advantage of him in the end. We had each other, though, and that was enough.

When I was a child, my parents made the difficult decision to move our family back to California, and then to Utah. We settled in a small town called Kanosh, with a population of around 350 people, and my dad started working on a ranch while my mother took a job at a hotel. As I began attending school, I didn't know any English, and this made me feel incredibly nervous, shy, and scared. I lacked confidence, and I struggled to even define that term! Every day, I would board the bus with trepidation, feeling isolated and alone. I couldn't understand anyone or even initiate a simple conversation for over a year, so I kept my head down and avoided eye contact with others.

Despite the challenges, the school offered a summer program to help me learn English up until the sixth grade, which proved to be immensely helpful. However, by the time I entered the third grade, my anxiety had escalated into full-blown panic attacks that required hospitalization, including one incident that required a three-hour drive to the University of Utah Hospital.

I Feel Like a Giant!

My parents, Ricardo and Lorena, were also struggling to adapt to a new country and new jobs while also trying to learn English, and the stress of the situation was almost too much for them to bear.

I remember being made fun of in the classroom. I was different, and I didn't want to be different. I felt like everyone was always talking about me, even though they probably were not. I would sit in class and look at the teachers and have no idea what they were saying. I did have some people come in and help me, and I felt a little bit more comfortable, but I was still so lost. I wanted to move back to California because it was a lot more diverse and there were a lot of teachers who spoke Spanish.

In the third grade, I finally began making friends, and their kindness made me feel so good! I remember a student even letting me copy her work, which was a huge relief. As I became more comfortable, I started getting invited to play with groups during recess, and my favorite activity was the monkey bars. Surprisingly, I wasn't even nervous the first time I tried them. Dancing became my passion as I grew older, but I struggled to learn the moves. I had to practice more than most because it was challenging for me to understand the rhythms and steps. As with most things, my hard work paid off as I excelled in the drill team throughout high school, and we even placed second at state three out of the four years that I attended.

Choice

Reflecting on those times, I have had a few traumatic experiences that have haunted me for years, and it took me a lifetime to learn to stand up and be strong when bad things happen in life. I know that when challenges happen in your life, you can always get back up when you feel you've reached rock bottom.

I fell in love a few times, just like most of us have, and each breakup was very difficult. And it was during this time, in my early adulthood, that I started to party. I started to drink and make foolish choices. I'm glad though that I started to go to school, and I graduated as a master esthetician. Although I seemed to have my life together on paper, it was a total roller coaster ride at the time. I caught myself moving back to my parent's home, as I tried to make better choices and find a better direction in life.

The state wrestling matches were going on, and that's a big deal in small towns because Millard County Wrestling was always a fan favorite. After the wrestling tournament, a group of us went to an after-party in Orem, Utah. I remember seeing a very handsome man standing across the room, laughing loudly and making everyone around him laugh along with him. He seemed like he was very well-liked and had a smile that was so perfectly white! I asked who he was, and my friends told me he was bad news, a player, and not to get caught up with him. After some time, Ryan and I passed each other on the staircase. He said "Hello" and I couldn't hide my

I Feel Like a Giant!

smile. I noticed he was not drinking, so I asked him if he drank. He said he was not because he was trying to be better, to improve his life and his plan was to go to Afghanistan. He ended up asking for my number, and we texted a few times, but that was all.

A year later, on my 22nd birthday, I received a message from Ryan saying, "One day, I am going to take you out."

I was living in West Jordan, Utah when Ryan and his unit returned from Afghanistan. I had no intention of hanging out with him until I passed him while he was out riding his motorcycle. I was with a friend and said, "Let's go hang out with Ryan and his friends."

Ryan was so nice! We hung out that night and I simply fell in love with his charm. I knew he was trouble, and my friends were right when they told me I shouldn't be hanging out with him, but I didn't want to change him or try to make him a better person; we just clicked. He would call me and ask if I wanted to go on a motorcycle ride, and I would tell him no because I just saw another girl on his bike! I wouldn't get jealous, because we were not dating but I would give him crap right back. We started to hang out more and more and built a good friendship. After three months of spending time as friends, Ryan kissed me. There was no going back.

I really enjoyed hanging out with Ryan, but he was always fighting with other people, and his anger would often get the best of him. He was not making very good choices, and I would have to help him pay his bills.

I remember we started to get really close, and one night I was over at his apartment when Ryan got the call that his little brother had rolled his car in the mountains, and tragically they found him frozen on the side of the road. They didn't know how long his brother was lying in the snow before the cops found him. Ryan said he and his little brother were best friends growing up. Now his brother was in a coma fighting for his life. It was a very difficult time, but I was glad I was there for him. Ryan would open up to me in a way I know he never does with anyone else, and I really enjoyed that special connection.

One day, I was not feeling very well, and shortly after taking a pregnancy test, I found out I was pregnant. I was hoping the cheap dollar tree pregnancy test was false, but it was true. There was no way I was ready. I was so heartbroken, and upset, and started to feel like my life was over. I called my friend and cousin for some advice, but no words could comfort me. At the time Ryan had started talking about possibly going back to Afghanistan, and also about going to a party with his friends in Lake Havasu. I had to tell him the news, but I didn't know how he would react. I showed up at his apartment, sat on his bed, and he asked if I wanted to go to Lake Havasu with him. I told him I couldn't go.

I Feel Like a Giant!

Later that night, I said, "I need to talk to you." I told him I was pregnant. To my surprise, he was overly excited and hugged me. He said, "I have been praying about our relationship because I am going back to Afghanistan, and this is an answer to my prayer." The next morning, Ryan told me he would be right back, but after a few hours, I received a phone call from my mom asking if I would like some food because she was sending food home with Ryan. I couldn't believe it! Ryan drove 1.5 hours away to tell my mom and dad he loved me and asked if we could get married. My parents had met Ryan a few times, but my dad thought he was a troublemaker when he showed up with a bullet bike and earrings in his ears! I had two little brothers that Ryan got along with pretty quickly because he loved sports just like them, and they both thought it was pretty cool he was in the military. Since then, my dad Ricardo has stated, "My life has been better now that Ryan is a part of it. He too, makes me feel like a giant - that I can accomplish anything! My dad and Ryan both play music and have built a great relationship over the years, and my mom says he is "My other son."

Back to me.

Saying "I do" is a choice.

Elizabeth and I took a trip to Las Vegas and dressed up very nicely. We had dinner at the Eiffel Tower, and that's where I did it. I got down on one knee and proposed. About two months later, we got married in Fillmore, Utah, in 2021 at the American Legion Hall. We were blessed to have family and friends from all over join in on the smiles and high-fives. Seeing my wife walk down the aisle between the wedding chairs that were set out for friends and family, I thought to myself, 'Wow, she is beautiful and man, this is really happening!' I felt so many different feelings. First, I felt very confident because I knew my wife was beautiful, smart, independent, hardworking, and comes from an amazing family. I also felt pretty awesome because I knew she was way out of my league! Before saying 'I do,' we both felt a sense of excitement and anticipation because we were looking forward to spending the rest of our lives together and making a public commitment to one another. We were still in the lovey-dovey stage where fighting and disagreements never happened in our marriage - lol! We both felt very nervous because I was leaving soon for Afghanistan, we had an unplanned child, and I, Ryan, was living a life of partying and sin before getting married. Although we loved each other, we both had the thought, "I hope we are not making a mistake." We were both a little nervous because everyone was staring right at us! After those thoughts melted away we were back to that feeling of happiness and contentment, knowing that we were about to marry the person we love. We felt gratitude before we said we shared those vows,' especially because we had supportive friends and family members who helped us plan a last-minute wedding and worked so hard to get us to this point.

When it comes to finding a potential romantic partner, having confidence can be an important factor. When you approach someone you're interested in, it's natural to feel nervous or uncertain about how they might respond. However, it's important to remember that confidence alone is not enough to build a healthy and fulfilling relationship. It's also important to prioritize things like mutual respect, open communication, and shared values when looking for a life partner. Being confident in yourself can help you feel more comfortable and secure as you navigate the dating world, but it's ultimately the connection you share with someone that will determine whether or not your relationship is successful in the long run.

Here are three quick tips to help boost your confidence when searching for a romantic partner:

- Firstly, always remain true to yourself and avoid imitating others. Authenticity and genuineness are key when it comes to attracting the right person. Don't feel the need to put on a façade or pretend to be someone else in order to impress someone. Instead, be open and honest about your interests, passions, and personality. Embrace who you are and what you enjoy, whether it's sports, books, or anything else.
- Secondly, it's important to accept yourself, even if you're not perfect. I mean, no one is! Don't focus on trying to be flawless but instead, strive to be the best

Choice

version of yourself. Remember that everyone has unique qualities that make them special, and it's important to be kind to others and take care of yourself. When you're comfortable in your own skin, you'll attract someone who appreciates you for who you are.

- Thirdly, when looking for a partner, it's crucial to consider what you want in a relationship. Think about the qualities and values you desire in a partner, and what kind of relationship you hope to have. Perhaps you're seeking someone who shares your interests or who is supportive and caring.

Chapter 2

One of a Kind

You are unique! Yes, there is only one of you in the whole world. Therefore, it's essential to be kind to yourself and talk to yourself positively. When you treat yourself well, you'll build self-esteem, confidence, and inner strength. Remember, you are one of a kind, and that's something to celebrate and cherish.

This is a lesson I learned in my relationship with Elizabeth. We faced many challenges during our marriage, but one of the most valuable lessons we learned is the importance of being kind to ourselves and talking to ourselves positively. When I came back from the war for the second time, I, like many others, was, unfortunately, struggling with PTSD and made poor choices that impacted our marriage and my health. But we didn't give up. Our journey to improve our relationship involved attending counseling sessions where we learned that we have the power to control our reactions and how we treat ourselves and each other.

We realized that being kind to ourselves and talking to ourselves positively can have a significant impact on our well-being and our relationship. We now make an effort to communicate effectively, express our love, spend quality time together, and apologize and forgive each other when we disagree. Although our marriage is not perfect, we choose to respond to challenges in a positive manner, and it has made all the difference!

By being kind to ourselves and talking to ourselves positively, we build a strong foundation of self-love and self-confidence that extends to all aspects of our lives. Sometimes, for some of us, it may be easier to show kindness to others and forget ourselves. Elizabeth and I believe that everyone should treat themselves with the same kindness and respect that they show to others. Remember, you are one of a kind, and you deserve to treat yourself with the same love and care that you give to those around you.

Inner Voice

We all have an inner voice that constantly talks to us. Sometimes it's positive, but often it's negative, critical, and self-defeating. Negative self-talk can be a serious problem, leading to anxiety, depression, and low self-esteem. But the good news is that we can train that inner voice, and we can learn to be kind to ourselves and talk to ourselves positively, which can help us become more positive and confident.

Being kind to yourself means treating yourself with the same care and compassion that you would show to a good friend. Instead of beating yourself up for your mistakes or flaws, you

I Feel Like a Giant!

acknowledge them and move on. You also give yourself credit for your strengths and accomplishments. When you are kind to yourself, you are more likely to feel positive emotions like happiness, contentment, and self-love.

Talking to yourself positively is a technique that can help you replace negative self-talk with more positive and empowering messages. It involves recognizing negative thoughts and replacing them with positive affirmations. For example, instead of saying "I'm so stupid" when you make a mistake, you can say "It's okay to make mistakes, I'll learn from this and do better next time." Positive self-talk can help improve your self-esteem and lead to more positive behaviors. It's very powerful!

One example of someone who has turned his life around through positive self-talk is Mike Tyson. Tyson was a world-famous boxer who experienced numerous setbacks and personal struggles throughout his career. However, he was able to overcome his negative self-talk and become a positive force in his own life. Tyson said that he used to tell himself he was "The best in the world" and that "No one can beat me." This positive self-talk helped him believe in himself and achieve great success in the ring.

But let's talk about the only one to beat Mike Tyson. Buster Douglas was a man on a mission. He had trained hard and was determined to defeat the reigning heavyweight champion, Mike Tyson. Despite the odds being against him, Buster

One of a Kind

believed in himself and his abilities. He was confident that he could win the fight, and he knew that his positive thinking and hard work would pay off.

Before the fight, Buster called his grandmother, who had always been a source of encouragement and inspiration for him. He told her about his upcoming match with Tyson, and how he was determined to come out on top. His grandmother listened intently, and then gave him a piece of advice that he would never forget.

"You just go in there and do your best," she said. "And if you lose, you come back and try again. But I know you can do it."

Buster was touched by his grandmother's words, and they gave him the strength and confidence he needed to face Tyson in the ring. As he stepped into the arena, he could feel the weight of the world on his shoulders. But he refused to let it get to him. He stayed focused on his goal, and he fought with all his heart.

The fight was intense from the start. Tyson was a fierce competitor, and he came at Buster with everything he had. But Buster was ready for him. He landed blow after blow, and he refused to back down. The rounds went by, and the two fighters were evenly matched.

In the eighth round, Buster landed a punch that sent Tyson reeling. The crowd roared as Tyson stumbled back, and Buster knew that he had the upper hand. He continued to

I Feel Like a Giant!

fight, and in the tenth round, he landed a punch that sent Tyson to the mat.

The crowd erupted into cheers as Buster was declared the winner. He had done it! He had beaten Mike Tyson. And as he celebrated his victory, he thought back to the conversation he had had with his grandmother before the fight. He knew that her words of encouragement had been the key to his success.

Buster's victory over Mike Tyson was a testament to his hard work, determination, and positive thinking thanks to his grandmother's words. Not only did he hear the words, he believed them, which makes all the difference in the world. He had believed in himself, and he had refused to give up. And in the end, he emerged victorious. It was a moment that he would never forget, and one that would inspire him for years to come.

Let me share another example of the inspiring, Oprah Winfrey. Winfrey has publicly spoken about how she uses positive affirmations to boost her confidence and achieve her goals. She has said that she repeats affirmations such as "I am worthy" and "I trust myself" to herself daily. This self-talk has helped her overcome obstacles and a very difficult past, and go on to become one of the most successful and influential women in the world.

There are many ways to practice being kind to yourself and talking to yourself positively.

One of a Kind

Here are some strategies you can try:

1. Start with self-compassion: When you make a mistake or fail at something, instead of being hard on yourself, acknowledge your feelings and treat yourself with kindness and understanding. This can help you bounce back and move forward with a positive attitude.

2. Focus on positive affirmations: Identify a few positive statements or affirmations that you can repeat to yourself when you need encouragement or motivation. Write them down and place them somewhere visible, such as on your bathroom mirror or computer desktop.

3. Practice gratitude: Take a few moments each day to reflect on the things you are grateful for. This can help you focus on the positive things in your life and feel more content.

4. Surround yourself with positivity: Seek out positive people, experiences, and environments that can help reinforce your positive self-talk and build your confidence.

5. Challenge negative thoughts: When you notice negative self-talk creeping in, challenge those thoughts with evidence to the contrary. For example, if you think "I'm not good enough," remind yourself of times when you have succeeded or received positive feedback.

I Feel Like a Giant!

Being kind to yourself and talking to yourself positively are powerful tools for developing a more positive outlook on life. By replacing negative self-talk with positive affirmations, we can improve our self-esteem, confidence, and overall well-being, just like Mike Tyson, Oprah Winfry and many others.

I remember one of my very first corporate events where I was invited to speak. It was held at the Grand America Hotel and attended by successful business owners from all over the United States. The tables were beautifully decorated, and the event was a grand affair. I was impressed with how well they treated me. Although I've been treated well at community events and school assemblies, there's something about being invited to a high-paying corporate event that sets it apart. You're expected to bring your knowledge, advice, and motivation to the table.

When I arrived, I was thrilled to see a large photo of myself and two other professional speakers on display. I was even more excited because I was the youngest of the speakers. Yet, when I took to the stage, I decided to do something different from my usual community events and school assemblies. I started my performance with a rap! Let's just say the older business people in the audience were not as enthusiastic as the younger crowds I was used to! After the song, I launched into my speech. Half of the audience enjoyed my story and found it entertaining, while the other half seemed less thrilled. I realized that I had misjudged the audience and should have prepared a less musical and more traditional speech. At that point in my career, I was gaining a lot of attention on social media for my music and storytelling, but I learned that day that people don't simply want to be entertained, they also want to be educated.

After my 60-minute performance, I didn't feel as confident as I usually did following an event. Normally, students and younger kids rush to the stage to speak with me, but I didn't get that here! The first person who approached me said, "I was once a drug addict and didn't learn anything from you." I was certainly caught off guard by his honesty and rawness! He was very successful and made sure to let me know. I tried to turn the situation around by saying a few clever things. I also told him that not everyone will appreciate your words or story, and we shook hands before he walked away. However, the negative comment stuck with me, and I couldn't stop thinking about it, even though there were positive comments from others who approached me afterwards.

After a few more people spoke with me, the meeting ended, and the lady who booked me was smiling and waving goodbye. However, the negative comment from earlier continued to bother me. I found myself actually bashing the man in my head and going into battle mode, which was wrong and only brought negativity into my soul! I realized that I needed to take my own advice and think positively. I called my wife, and she supported me like a mother supporting her son against a bully. It was reassuring to have my best friend's support.

I Feel Like a Giant!

As I drove home, I thought about how this was my first corporate event, and I hadn't known what to expect. My wife's words replayed in my head, reminding me to think positively. I asked myself if there was any truth to the man's comments, and I realized that he was right. I needed to do more than just sing and tell stories; I needed to educate people. That was what they were there for.

Over the next six months, I wrote a book, staying up for hours with the man's comments replaying in my mind. I wrote down the five steps to Conquering Your Colosseum. The book was titled "Conquering Your Colosseum" but unfortunately, I accidentally deleted the book twice! But I was so determined to one day be an Amazon bestseller that I wrote it again with the thought "God knew it was not good enough and I needed to try again." In 2022, my book sold hundreds of copies in the first three days thanks to my social media family and was at number 1 on Amazon! I learned during this experience and many others that when someone says something hurtful to us, it's natural to feel upset or discouraged. But instead of letting those negative words bring us down, we can use them as motivation to become stronger and more determined and to step back and ask whether there is any truth in the words that are useful.

By using hurtful words as fuel for our inner fire, we can channel our emotions in a positive way and prove to ourselves and others that we are capable of great things. It's important to remember that we have the power to choose how we react to negative words, and we can choose to use them as a stepping stone towards success and personal growth.

Friendship

We all want to have friends who support and defend us, but sometimes people say mean things behind our backs. It happens. It's normal to feel upset, but how we react can impact the relationship. If we confront the person aggressively, it could make things worse. Instead, we should try to understand *why* they said those things and talk to them respectfully.

As we get older, we realize that people who talk badly about us may have their own issues, like jealousy or insecurity, and that it is rarely about us. Knowing this allows us to have compassion for the other person, and helps us feel less angry at the situation.

Having said that, we should aim to surround ourselves with people who make us feel good and who we can have conversations with that help us grow and feel better.

Friendships can be tricky, but by being kind and understanding, we can build deeper connections with our friends.

Elizabeth:

When Ryan left for Afghanistan, it was hard because he was my lover and best friend. When you fall in love and move to

I Feel Like a Giant!

a new place and all of your friends are away from you, you have to re-evaluate your life. Luckily for me, I had a job working at a dentist's office, and my parents helped me with our firstborn. I was back in my hometown and had some great friends around me. It can be a little challenging to make the change from being a young single adult to being a parent! My friends and I would get together, but with kids now, jobs, and the life and responsibilities of being a parent, it's definitely something you have to grow into, and you never stop growing.

After Ryan came home, we moved a few times in the next few years and always tried to be kind and make new friends. Ryan is very outgoing, and he will talk to anyone - even if they are the silent type! We would make friends, but then subsequently we'd find out that those people are not the same people to our faces. Not a good feeling! This is something that has always bothered me. Why can't people just be nice, and honest?

I know Ryan and I are not perfect, but we make sure to correct each other when we say things that can hurt other people's feelings or things that we wouldn't want them to hear us say behind their backs. Instead, we choose to try and be kind to everyone, have a small circle of quality friends, and look for opportunities to help others. Even when some people are quick to ask for advice, they may be slow to give us the answers that would help us in return. However, we still strive to maintain a positive attitude and to be helpful to others whenever possible even if they don't particularly like us! Some advice that has stuck with me for a long time, was given by one of Ryan's friends. He told him once that when people talk badly about you, ask yourself if there is any truth to what they are saying and be honest about it. Although we shouldn't speak badly about others, sometimes hearing those things may provide the motivation we need to change something about ourselves or confront those people. Just like Ryan learned at that first corporate event.

Our Children

Children are always watching and learning from the adults around them. It's important to remember that kids will follow your example, instead of your advice. This is a hard lesson for a parent to hear! This means that it's not enough to simply tell children what to do or how to behave, but rather to model the behaviors and values that we want them to emulate. Not always easy! But remember, if you are not being kind to yourself and talking to yourself positively, your children will follow your lead and think that it's normal to be unkind to themselves, which is the last thing we'd want for them.

For example, if you want your child to be honest, you need to model honesty by being truthful with them and others. If you want your child to be respectful, you need to model respect by treating others with kindness and courtesy. If you want your child to have a strong work ethic, you need to model hard work by putting effort and dedication into your own job or responsibilities.

It's not just about what you say, but what you do. Yes, children are always watching and observing, even when we don't realize it. They learn by example, and the behaviors and values that we model will have a significant impact on their development and character. I know it's a big responsibility and no one is perfect. We can only do our best and apologise when we make mistakes and use those times as opportunities for learning.

So, it's important to be mindful of our own behavior and to make a conscious effort to model positive behaviors and values. By doing so, we can help shape our children's attitudes and behaviors in a positive way, setting them up for success both now and in the future.

Wishing to be a Public Speaker

Ryan:

In 2017, I received an unexpected invitation to speak at a high school on Veterans Day. Little did I know that this opportunity would propel me into a career as a motivational speaker, taking me around the world to share my story!

During my eight-minute speech, I shared my life struggles and the hardships I had faced, highlighting the importance of perseverance and resilience in the face of adversity. I reminded the students that everyone experiences struggles and challenges throughout their lives, but it's these very struggles that build the strengths necessary to succeed.

One of a Kind

I also spoke about the sacrifices made by the brave men and women who go to battle to protect our opportunities to grow up in a land full of possibilities and freedom. Their courage and selflessness serve as inspiration for us all, reminding us to make the most of every opportunity we are given.

The audience was captivated, and I could sense a palpable energy in the room. It was great! After the speech, the applause was thunderous, confirming that my message had resonated with the students.

Buoyed by this success, I resolved to pursue speaking opportunities with renewed vigor. I practiced my speeches relentlessly, even in unconventional settings such as baseball fields and rodeo arenas, envisioning a future where I would speak to thousands of people.

Despite my struggles with PTSD and ADHD, I persevered, determined to overcome any obstacles in my path. I refused to let my self-doubt and insecurity hold me back, instead choosing to channel my fears into motivation and inspiration for others.

Today, I am proud to have achieved my dream of becoming one of the most sought-after youth motivational speakers in the United States of America! My journey has been challenging, but it has taught me the value of hard work, persistence, and resilience. I hope my story serves as an inspiration to others, reminding them that the struggles and hardships we face are often stepping stones to our future success.

A Story That Motivated Me

I used to work out at the small gym in Delta, Utah with my wife Elizabeth, and she would always feed me healthy foods and push me on. She knew I could achieve my goals and encouraged me endlessly. Besides my wife's support, I would also listen to a video and a story by Eric Thomas, which also inspired me. It goes like this:

"How Bad Do You Want It?" by Eric Thomas

There was a young man who wanted to make a lot of money, so he went to a guru and told him, "I want to be on the same level as you." The guru replied, "If you want to be on my level, meet me tomorrow at the beach." The young man arrived at the beach at 4 am, dressed in a suit, but the guru took his hand and asked him, "How bad do you want to be successful?" The young man answered, "Real bad." The guru instructed him to walk out into the water, and the young man followed him, going waist-deep into the water. But he became frustrated and exclaimed that he wanted to make money, not be a lifeguard! The guru told him to walk a little further until the water reached his shoulders, and then his mouth. The young man wanted to go back to the shore, but the guru said, "When you want to succeed as badly as you want to, breathe, then you will be successful." The guru held the young man's head underwater until he was about to pass out and then asked him how badly he wanted success. The young man realized that he needed to want it as much as he wanted to breathe. The guru explained that most people only 'kind of want to be successful and would rather party, sleep or be cool instead of working hard for success. To be successful,' and that you must be willing to sacrifice sleep and work with only a few hours of sleep. The guru emphasized that you must want it so badly that you're willing to stay awake for three days straight because missing an opportunity for success is not an option.

When I was striving for success, I spent hours watching and listening to speeches by Eric Thomas. I was inspired by the man in the videos who had achieved so much. While working at a chemical plant and serving in the Utah National Guard, I also spoke and worked at a group adolescent home to earn enough money to further achieve our goals and dreams. My wife and I always worked together to make it all possible.

However, during this time, I struggled secretly with anger outbursts and PTSD episodes. I would wake up in the middle of the night, looking for the enemy and having bad dreams about war. I didn't understand what was happening to me, and it was a constant cycle of feeling like everything was going well one minute, and then doing crazy things the next, even when I was trying to be a champion.

The words of others helped me during these difficult times and reminded me to speak kindly to myself, work hard, and be good to myself. In my book, "Conquering Your

I Feel Like a Giant!

Colosseum," I share more about these stories. It wasn't easy, but with perseverance and determination, my wife and I were able to achieve our goals and make our dreams a reality. I had to *want success as badly as I wanted to breathe.*

Life can be full of challenges, from mental health struggles to the all-common work-life balance, and it's important to remember that you're not alone. One way to boost your confidence and feel more capable of overcoming obstacles is by cultivating a positive mindset and practicing self-compassion. When you speak kindly to yourself and focus on your strengths and accomplishments, you'll likely feel more confident and empowered to tackle difficult situations.

On the other hand, negative self-talk can erode your self-confidence and make it so much harder to cope with setbacks. That's where the analogy of the glass comes in: if you fill an empty glass with muddy water (representing negative self-talk), the water will stay murky and unappealing. But if you pour in clear water (representing positive self-talk and words of affirmation) regularly, over time, the muddy water will be displaced and the glass will become clearer.

Of course, building confidence isn't just about changing your internal dialogue. Seeking support from others, whether it's from friends, family, or professionals, can also be a helpful way to manage mental health issues and other challenges. You don't need to struggle or face challenges alone and tough it out! And when setbacks or failures happen (as they inevitably will), it's important to view them as opportunities for growth and learning rather than as reflections of your worth or potential.

In summary, a positive mindset and self-compassion can make you more confident and better equipped to navigate life's challenges. Remember, you are one of a kind. There is no one in the world like you, so be the best version of yourself. By taking care of yourself and seeking support when needed, you can cultivate resilience and strength, no matter what obstacles come your way.

Chapter 3

Nutritious Eating and Exercising

We all want to feel confident in our own skin, but it's not always easy to achieve. But taking care of our bodies through regular exercise and healthy eating habits can be a powerful tool in boosting our confidence levels. Not only do these habits make us look and feel better, but research has shown that they can also help us perform better in all areas of our lives.

The Benefits of Regular Exercise

When we exercise, our bodies release endorphins, which are natural mood-boosting chemicals. They're great! This leads to an immediate improvement in our mood and energy levels, which can have a positive impact on our self-confidence. Additionally, regular exercise has been shown to improve our overall physical health, including reducing our risk of chronic diseases such as heart disease and diabetes.

But the benefits of exercise go beyond just physical health. Exercise has also been linked to improved cognitive function, including increased creativity and problem-solving abilities. This means that by exercising regularly, we can not only look and feel better but also perform better in our work and personal lives.

The Importance of a Balanced Diet

In addition to regular exercise, maintaining a balanced diet is key to improving our confidence levels. A diet that is rich in whole foods such as fruits, vegetables, and lean proteins can help improve our overall physical health, leading to a more positive self-image. Eating a balanced diet can also help regulate our energy levels, reducing the likelihood of mood swings or energy crashes that can negatively impact our self-confidence.

Furthermore, studies have shown that a healthy diet can improve cognitive function, including memory and concentration. This means that by eating a balanced diet, we can improve our mental acuity and perform better in all areas of our lives. All of these elements add up to a healthier and happier individual that performs better in all areas of their life.

Putting it all Together

By combining regular exercise with a balanced diet, we can achieve the ultimate goal of improved self-confidence. Not only will we look and feel better physically, but we will also be better equipped to handle the demands of our daily lives. Whether it's at work or in our personal relationships, we will have the energy and mental clarity to perform at our best, to be able to handle the tough situations that come our way, which will in turn lead to even greater levels of self-confidence.

Mental Health

In addition to improving your physical appearance, exercise can also have a positive effect on your mental health. Regular exercise has been shown to reduce stress and anxiety levels, which can have a major impact on your confidence levels. When you are less stressed and anxious, you are more likely to feel positive and self-assured and handle situations with calm and ease.

Exercise can also help you get better sleep, which is crucial for your mental health. When you get enough restorative sleep, you wake up feeling refreshed and energized, which can have a positive impact on your confidence levels. On the other hand, when you are sleep-deprived, you can feel irritable, tired, and insecure. Everything is harder! By helping you get better sleep, exercise can boost your confidence levels.

A Few Steps I Use to Get Started with Exercising and Eating Healthily:

1. Set Realistic Goals

The first step to getting started with exercising and eating healthily is to set realistic goals. Be specific about what you want to achieve, such as running a 5K or losing 10 pounds.

Make sure your goals are achievable and set a timeline for achieving them.

2. Start Slow

It's important to start slow when beginning an exercise routine or changing your eating habits. Trying to do too much too soon can lead to burnout or injury. Begin with small changes, such as taking a 10-minute walk every day or swapping out one unhealthy snack for a healthier option. According to the World Health Organization, engaging in at least 150 minutes of moderate-intensity exercise per week can reduce the risk of cardiovascular diseases, diabetes, and some cancers.

I remember not exercising for a few months and really letting my diet go to crap! I started on the treadmill with one mile a day, and after two days, I was feeling confident and told my wife we should do a marathon! That day, I tried to run four miles, and my back was giving out at three miles and I got a foot injury way before the four-mile mark! I learned the hard way that I am no longer a seven-year-old who can wake up and run around the playground for hours on end.

Elizabeth says, "After giving birth in particular, you feel like you don't want to go to the gym because you're tired."

After giving birth, many women experience physical and emotional changes that can make it difficult to find the motivation to exercise. Lack of sleep, hormonal changes, and the demands of caring for a newborn can all contribute to fatigue and a lack of energy. Simply drinking a whole hot cup of coffee can be a challenge, let alone a gym workout.

However, regular exercise can actually really help new moms regain their energy and improve their overall physical and mental health. Exercise can help reduce stress, improve mood, and increase stamina. It's important to start slowly and listen to your body, especially if you're recovering from a cesarean section or other delivery complications, but it's really worth getting started in little steps.

If going to the gym feels overwhelming, there are plenty of other ways to incorporate exercise into your daily routine such as taking a brisk walk with your baby in a stroller, doing gentle yoga or stretching at home, or attending a postnatal exercise class are all great options.

It's important to remember that it's okay to take things slowly and prioritize rest and recovery in the early postpartum period. With time, patience, and a commitment to self-care, new moms can regain their energy and feel confident in their ability to exercise and care for their new baby.

3.Find Activities You Enjoy

One of the biggest challenges when starting an exercise routine is staying motivated over the long term. One way to overcome this challenge is to find activities that you truly enjoy. When you find something that you love to do, exercise can become a fun and rewarding experience rather than a chore.

There are countless types of physical activities to choose from, so it's important to find something that suits your interests and fits your lifestyle. If you love spending time outdoors, hiking, biking, or swimming might be great options for you. If you enjoy socializing and being part of a team, consider joining a sports league or taking a dance class.

The key is to experiment and try different activities until you find something that you genuinely enjoy. Once you've found an activity that you love, make it a regular part of your routine. This will not only help you stay motivated and committed to your exercise goals but can also lead to other positive changes in your life, such as improved mood, better sleep, and increased energy levels.

4. Make Healthy Eating a Habit

In today's fast-paced world, it can be difficult to find the time and resources to prepare healthy meals. Many people turn to processed and convenience foods, which are often high in calories, sugar, and unhealthy fats. However, with a little effort and planning, it is possible to find and prepare meals made with real, whole ingredients.

One strategy is to focus on fresh, whole foods that are in season and readily available. This might include fruits and vegetables, lean protein sources like chicken or fish, whole grains, and healthy fats like avocado and nuts. Look for recipes that use these ingredients and experiment with different flavors and cooking techniques.

Another approach is to plan and prepare ahead of time. This can help you save time and ensure that you have healthy meals on hand when you need them, and avoid the extra stress of figuring out what to cook each day. Start by setting aside a few hours each week to plan out your meals and grocery shop. Cook large batches of protein, grains, and veggies that can be combined in different ways throughout the week.

Finally, consider joining a meal delivery service that specializes in healthy, real food. These services can provide you with fresh, pre-made meals that are tailored to your dietary needs and preferences. While these services can be more expensive than cooking your meals at home, they can be a convenient and time-saving option for those with busy lifestyles.

Remember, finding and preparing healthy meals takes time and effort, but it is an investment in your health and well-being for you and your whole family. With a little creativity and planning, you can enjoy delicious, nourishing meals made with real, whole ingredients.

Get Support

Having a support system can be a crucial factor in maintaining your exercise and healthy eating goals. One way to find support is by joining a fitness class, finding a workout partner, or seeking out a support group. Being surrounded by

Nutritious Eating and Exercising

others who share similar goals can provide accountability, motivation and fun! It's important to note that when you start to shift your mindset and goals, not all of your friends may want to join you on your journey, and that's okay. You can always find new friends within a gym community. As you establish a routine, you'll likely see familiar faces who attend the gym at the same time as you. Additionally, most people at the gym are there to feel good about themselves and often enjoy friendly interactions with others. This sense of community can turn your gym experience into a small family. By following these tips, you can embark on a journey to improve confidence through regular exercise and healthy eating habits. Remember to take it slow, make it enjoyable, and seek support along the way. With time and consistency, you'll soon notice positive changes in both your body and mind.

Years ago, when my wife and I were inspired by the importance of eating clean and working out, we met a man named David Goggins. His book, 'Can't Hurt Me: Master Your Mind and Defy the Odds,' is the story of David Goggins. Goggins grew up in a difficult environment and faced numerous challenges throughout his life. He struggled with obesity and asthma as a child and was also subjected to racism. Eventually, he decided to take control of his life and started training to become a Navy SEAL.

When he first went to the Navy SEAL recruiter's office, he was told that he was too overweight to join. At the time, Goggins weighed over 300 pounds, and the recruiter laughed

I Feel Like a Giant!

at him when he expressed interest in becoming a SEAL. However, Goggins was determined to prove everyone wrong, and he spent months training and working on his fitness. Months later, Goggins returned to the recruiter's office and tried out for the SEALS. Despite facing numerous obstacles during training, including a fractured knee and severe shin splints, he refused to give up. He eventually graduated from SEAL training and went on to serve in the military for several years. He achieved his goal!

Throughout his career as a SEAL and later as an endurance athlete, Goggins has emphasized the importance of mental toughness and pushing yourself beyond your limits. He has set numerous endurance records, including running 100 miles in under 24 hours and completing the Badwater 135 ultramarathon, which covers 135 miles through Death Valley in California.

In terms of healthy eating and exercise, Goggins is a strong advocate for both. He believes that what you put into your body is just as important as how you train it. He has talked about the importance of fueling your body with healthy, nutrient-dense foods and avoiding processed foods and sugar. He also emphasizes the importance of hydration and recommends drinking plenty of water throughout the day.

In terms of exercise, Goggins believes in pushing yourself to your limits and constantly challenging yourself to improve. He recommends incorporating a variety of different exercises into your routine, including strength training, cardio, and mobility work. He also stresses the importance of rest and recovery and recommends taking rest days and getting plenty of sleep to allow your body to recover and repair.

After listening to and reading his book, we learned that there are no excuses; it's just about doing what you don't want to do most of the time! David Goggins has acknowledged that there are days when he doesn't feel like eating healthily or working out. However, he believes that it's important to push through those feelings and do what needs to be done. He says that "motivation is crap" and that it's all about discipline and doing what you need to do, even when you don't feel like it. Goggins also emphasizes the importance of building habits and routines that make it easier to stick to healthy habits even on days when motivation is lacking.

In summary, it's clear that making positive lifestyle changes, such as exercising regularly and eating a healthy diet, is essential for not only improving physical health but also boosting self-esteem and confidence. To avoid burnout or injury, it's important to start small and gradually build up to a sustainable routine. The World Health Organization recommends at least 150 minutes of moderate-intensity exercise per week to reduce the risk of chronic diseases. By prioritizing exercise and healthy eating habits in your daily routine, you can achieve your health goals and live a happier, more fulfilling life. So, let's all remember to take care of ourselves by exercising and eating good, healthy nutritious foods.

Chapter 4

Fail Forward - Be Brave Enough to Fail

Fearlessness is not the absence of fear, but rather the willingness to confront our fears and overcome them. It requires us to have confidence in ourselves, our abilities, and our capacity to handle whatever challenges come our way.

While celebrities and singers get all the attention, it's important to remember that not everyone wants to be famous. There are countless unsung heroes in industries across the nation who wake up every day, take risks, and try new things. These individuals exhibit fearlessness and push through their fears of failure to achieve success. Here are just a few examples:

1. Single parents, young parents, and students: these individuals exhibit fearlessness on a daily basis as they navigate the challenges of raising children or pursuing an education while facing financial or personal obstacles. They push through their fears and prioritize the well-being and future success of themselves and their loved ones.

2. Architecture and engineering: professionals in these fields are tasked with designing and building structures that are safe, functional, and aesthetically pleasing. They must overcome their fears of potential design flaws or construction issues and push through the complex and often stressful process of bringing their creations to life.

3. Arts, culture, and entertainment: musicians, actors, writers, and other artists often face rejection, criticism, and uncertainty in their careers. They must push through their fears of failure or rejection and continue to pursue their passions, even when faced with setbacks.

4. Business, management, and administration: leaders in these fields must make tough decisions that can impact the success of their organizations. They must push through their fears of making mistakes or being criticized and have the courage to take calculated risks and implement new ideas.

5. Communications: professionals in this field must often overcome their fear of public speaking or presenting ideas to a large audience. They must have the courage to speak up and communicate their ideas effectively, even when faced with difficult or sensitive topics.

6. Community and social services: individuals working in these fields often face challenging situations and must have the fearlessness to advocate for their clients and stand up for what is right. They must also have the

courage to confront difficult situations, such as domestic violence or homelessness, and work towards finding solutions.

7. Education: teachers and administrators must have the fearlessness to take risks and try new teaching methods or approaches, even when faced with resistance or criticism. They must also have the courage to advocate for their students and work towards providing them with the best possible education.

8. Science and technology: professionals in these fields must push through their fears of failure and continue to experiment and innovate in order to make new discoveries and advancements. They must also have the courage to speak out and stand up for scientific integrity and ethical practices.

9. Installation, repair, and maintenance: workers in these fields often face dangerous or physically demanding tasks, such as working at great heights or in confined spaces. They must have the fearlessness to work through these challenges and prioritize safety while still getting the job done.

10. Farming, fishing, and forestry: these industries require workers to face unpredictable weather, physical labor, and the dangers of working with heavy machinery or in remote locations. Workers must have the courage to persist through these challenges and provide for their families and communities.

11. Government: officials must make difficult decisions and policies that can impact the lives of millions of people. They must push through their fears of criticism or unpopularity and have the courage to stand up for what they believe is right and just.

12. Health and medicine: healthcare professionals must push through their fears of working with critically ill or injured patients and making life-or-death decisions. They must have the courage to advocate for their patients and provide compassionate care, even in difficult situations.

13. Law and public policy: professionals in these fields must have the fearlessness to stand up for justice and fairness, even in the face of opposition or controversy. They must also have the courage to speak out against injustice and advocate for marginalized or vulnerable populations.

14. Sales: salespeople must push through their fears of rejection and failure in order to build relationships with clients and close deals. They must have the courage to persist through difficult negotiations and handle rejection with grace and professionalism.

15. It's important to recognize that many immigrants come to a new country seeking a better future for themselves and their families. It takes a great deal of bravery to leave behind everything familiar and start anew in a foreign land, often with limited resources and without knowledge of the language or culture. For instance, my father-in-law and mother-in-law,

I Feel Like a Giant!

Ricardo and Lorena Martinez, moved to the United States without speaking English and worked tirelessly to create a better life for their family. They even welcomed me into their family when I married their daughter, Elizabeth.

Our ancestors similarly faced countless obstacles and challenges but persevered to build a better future for us. Their unwavering resilience and determination can serve as a source of inspiration for us when we encounter difficulties. With their guidance and our own inner strength, we can overcome any hurdles and make a positive impact in the world. Let us honor the sacrifices and contributions of immigrants, past and present, and strive to create a better future for ourselves and future generations.

Now let's go back to a few people we have heard of, movies we have seen, or books we have read that have a positive outlook on failing forward.

"The Pursuit of Happiness" is a biographical drama film based on the life of Chris Gardner, a struggling salesman who became homeless with his young son, Christopher, in San Francisco during the early 1980s.

In the movie, Will Smith plays the role of Chris Gardner, who is determined to make a better life for himself and his son despite facing numerous challenges and setbacks. After losing his job as a salesman, Chris takes on an unpaid internship at a stock brokerage firm, hoping to secure a full-time position that will enable him to provide for his family.

Throughout the film, Chris faces many obstacles, including financial difficulties, homelessness, and the stress of being a single parent. However, he never gives up on his dream of a better life for himself and his son, and he continues to work hard and persevere through every challenge that comes his way.

One of the most inspiring moments in the film is when Chris and his son are forced to spend the night in a subway station bathroom. Despite feeling hopeless and defeated, Chris still wakes up early the next morning and takes his son to a meeting, determined to impress his potential employers and secure a job.

Throughout the film, Chris embodies the concept of failing forward. He experiences many setbacks and failures along the way, but he never gives up on his goal of providing a better life for his family. Instead, he uses each failure as an opportunity to learn and grow, and he remains focused on his goal even when things seem impossible.

In the end, Chris's hard work and perseverance pay off, and he is offered a full-time position at the brokerage firm. The film serves as a powerful reminder of the importance of never giving up on your dreams, even in the face of adversity.

I Feel Like a Giant!

The "Pursuit of Happiness" resonates with many Americans today because it depicts the struggles and hardships that many people face in their pursuit of success and happiness.

The movie shows the difficulties of being a single parent, dealing with financial instability, and facing repeated failures in the pursuit of a better life.

Like Chris Gardner in the movie, many people are forced to work long hours, make sacrifices, and take risks in order to pursue their dreams.

Being fearless doesn't mean that you will never fail, but it does mean that you will keep trying until you succeed. It means having the courage to take the first step towards your dreams, even if it feels uncomfortable or uncertain.

One person I know you would all love is <u>Les Brown,</u> who is a true inspiration to anyone who has ever faced adversity in their life. Despite experiencing countless setbacks and obstacles, Les has always held fast to his belief that "It's not over until I win." This unwavering determination has been the driving force behind his success and has inspired countless others to keep pushing forward in the face of adversity.

Les' story is a testament to the power of the human spirit. Born into poverty and abandoned by his mother at a young age, he was labeled as "educable mentally retarded" in school. He was told he would never amount to anything and faced numerous obstacles throughout his life.

Fail Forward - Be Brave Enough to Fail

At the age of 18, Les found himself homeless and sleeping on the floor of his friend's office. He had no job, no money, and no direction in life. He would scavenge for food in garbage cans and sleep in abandoned buildings. One day, he stumbled upon a speech given by Zig Ziglar that changed his life forever. Ziglar's message about the power of positive thinking and self-belief inspired Les to turn his life around.

He continued to work hard and to believe in himself, even when no one else did.

Eventually, Les's hard work paid off. He became a highly sought-after motivational speaker, inspiring people around the world with his messages of hope, perseverance, and success. He has written several books, including "Live Your Dreams" and "It's Not Over Until You Win," which have become bestsellers.

Les Brown's story is a testament to the power of perseverance, determination, and faith. He overcame tremendous obstacles to achieve his dreams and has inspired countless others to do the same. His message is simple, yet powerful: it's not over until you win. No matter what challenges you face, no matter how many times you fall, you can always get back up and keep moving forward.

Now, my wife and I are brainstorming on other amazing movies with women actresses, and we both love the movie with Jennifer Lopez in it, "Enough". This movie tells the story of a woman named Slim, played by Jennifer Lopez, who

I Feel Like a Giant!

is trapped in an abusive relationship with her wealthy husband. As the abuse escalates, Slim decides to take matters into her own hands and fight back to protect herself and her daughter.

Slim's journey can be seen as another example of failing forward. Initially, she tries to keep the peace and make things work with her husband, despite his abusive behavior. However, she realizes that this approach is not working and decides to take action. Along the way, Slim encounters obstacles and setbacks, such as being hunted down by her husband's hired thugs and struggling to make ends meet while in hiding.

Despite these challenges, Slim does not give up. Instead, she continues to push forward, learning new skills such as self-defense and honing her instincts to stay one step ahead of her husband's men. She also seeks out help and support from others, such as her friend and fellow abuse survivor, and does not let pride or fear get in the way of her journey.

In the end, Slim is able to confront her husband and triumph over her abuser, but this victory does not come without a price. She is forced to confront the painful reality of her past and the toll that the abuse has taken on her and her daughter. Despite this, she is able to move forward and find a new sense of strength and independence.

Overall, "Enough" is a powerful example of how failing forward is not about avoiding challenges or setbacks, but rather about embracing them as opportunities to learn, grow, and ultimately overcome. Slim's journey shows us that even in the darkest of times, it is possible to find the courage and resilience to keep moving forward towards a better future.

While "Enough" is about a woman named Slim who is escaping an abusive husband, the message of falling forward is universal and can be applied to anyone facing difficult situations.

Many people, both men and women, can relate to the struggle of facing abuse or other difficult circumstances. Like Slim, they may feel trapped or powerless, but the message of falling forward reminds us that we are never truly stuck. By taking small steps towards a better future, even in the face of obstacles, we can make progress and eventually reach our goals.

Moreover, the movie highlights the importance of self-care and self-defense, not just physically but also emotionally and mentally. It shows how we can empower ourselves by learning self-defense techniques and seeking support from those around us. It also reminds us that it's okay to reach out for help when we need it, whether it's from friends, family, or professionals.

The Creed movies are about the journey of Adonis Creed, son of legendary boxer Apollo Creed, who wants to make a name for himself in the boxing world. The movies show Adonis facing many challenges and obstacles, both in his personal

I Feel Like a Giant!

life and in the boxing ring, but he never gives up and continues to push forward, despite the odds against him.

Like their predecessor "Rocky," the Creed movies are known for their inspirational stories of overcoming obstacles and succeeding against all odds as he navigates the world of professional boxing and comes to terms with his family legacy.

Adonis struggles to find his place in the world, feeling like he's always living in the shadow of his father's greatness. Despite the objections of his father's former rival and friend, Rocky Balboa, Adonis trains relentlessly to become a boxer, determined to make a name for himself. Along the way, he faces many setbacks and obstacles, but with the help of Rocky and his own unwavering determination, he finally earns his shot at the title. The movie reminds us that success is not handed to us, but must be earned through hard work and perseverance.

"Creed II" picks up where the first movie left off, with Adonis now the heavyweight champion of the world. However, he soon learns that being a champion is not enough to satisfy his thirst for greatness. When he's challenged by Viktor Drago, the son of the man who killed his father in the ring, Adonis must confront his past. Once again, he faces many obstacles, both physical and emotional, but he refuses to give up, knowing that his journey is about more than just winning a boxing match. This film highlights the importance of confronting our past and learning from our mistakes, even when it's difficult.

Both movies also delve into the theme of family and how it can both support and hinder us on our journey to success. Adonis has to learn to balance his own desires and goals with his responsibilities to his family, both the one he was born into and the one he has created with his girlfriend. Through his struggles, we see the importance of having a support system, but also the necessity of forging our own path and making our own choices.

Overall, the Creed movies are emotional and inspiring tales of resilience, determination, and the pursuit of greatness. They remind us that success is not always about winning, but about pushing ourselves to be our best selves and never giving up, even when the odds are against us.

The Story of David and Goliath: A Metaphor for Overcoming Personal Challenges and Embracing Failure

The story of David and Goliath is a famous biblical tale from the Old Testament. It tells the story of a young shepherd boy named David who, through faith and courage, defeated a giant Philistine warrior named Goliath.

According to the story, the Philistines and Israelites were engaged in a long-standing battle. The Philistines had a giant warrior named Goliath who challenged the Israelites to send out a champion to fight him in single combat. None of the

I Feel Like a Giant!

Israelite soldiers dared to face Goliath, who was over nine feet tall and heavily armed!

David, who was not yet a soldier, but a shepherd boy, came to the Israelite camp to deliver supplies to his brothers who were part of the army. When he heard Goliath's challenge, he volunteered to fight the giant, claiming that he had faith in God and that the Lord would protect him.

King Saul, impressed by David's courage, gave him permission to face Goliath, and he was provided with armor and weapons. However, David refused to wear them, instead relying on his trusty slingshot and a few smooth stones he had picked up from a nearby stream. Her certainly was confident and his faith was strong!

As Goliath approached, David ran toward him, slung a stone, and hit Goliath on the forehead, causing him to fall to the ground. David then used Goliath's own sword to behead him, proving to the Philistines that God was with the Israelites.

David's story is one of bravery and determination in the face of daunting challenges. He faced the giant warrior, Goliath, with no armor or experience, yet he believed in himself and his abilities to overcome the odds. He knew there was a high chance of failure, but regardless, he was still willing to try.

Similarly, we may encounter personal challenges that seem insurmountable, but we can learn from David's courage and willingness to embrace failure. We can be confident in our abilities and use the tools at our disposal to overcome these challenges. We can believe in ourselves and our capacity to overcome obstacles, even if we fail along the way, and in the end, our achievements can make us feel like a giant - no matter how big or small we are!

I mentioned earlier that I'm on the short side, but believe me, when I feel great, when I feel things are falling into place and when I'm believing in myself and my abilities, I do 'feel like a giant!'

David's story also teaches us the importance of embracing failure. He did not know if he would win or lose, but he was willing to take the risk and face his fears. Similarly, we should not be afraid to fail in our own lives, as failure is often a necessary part of growth and learning. We can learn so much from our mistakes and use them as opportunities to improve ourselves and become stronger.

In addition, David's faith in God helped him overcome his fear and doubt. We can find comfort and strength in our own faith, whatever form that takes, to help us face challenges with courage and resilience.

In summary, the story of David and Goliath can serve as a powerful metaphor for overcoming personal challenges and embracing failure. We can be confident like David, (even a giant!) using the tools and resources at our disposal to win the battle, even if we fail along the way. We can believe in ourselves, find strength in our faith, and emerge victorious in our own lives, no matter the outcome.

I know you guys can feel like a giant too!

Some Advice For Parents

As parents, we all want to set a good example for our children. We want to teach them how to be successful, happy, and resilient. But what about when we fail? What do we do then? Do we try to hide our mistakes and pretend everything is perfect? Or do we acknowledge our failures and show our children how to fail forward? I think you know the answer to that!

Failing forward means turning setbacks into opportunities. It means learning from our mistakes and using that knowledge to grow and improve. It means not giving up when things get tough, but instead, pushing through and coming out stronger on the other side. This is a valuable lesson for children to learn, and parents have a unique opportunity to teach it.

As we know, children are always watching and learning from their parents. They see how we react to success and failure, and they internalize those lessons. If we try to hide our failures, our children will learn that failure is something to be ashamed of. They may be afraid to take risks and try new things because they don't want to fail. This can limit their potential and prevent them from reaching their goals and show them that giving up early is normal.

If we embrace our failures and show our children how to fail forward, we can show them that failure is a natural part of the learning process and that it's okay to make mistakes. We can teach them resilience and perseverance, and help them develop a growth mindset that will serve them well throughout their lives.

It's not always easy to fail forward, especially when we feel like we've let ourselves or our children down. But if we can show them how to turn failures into opportunities, we can help them develop the confidence and resilience they need to navigate life's challenges.

So, how can parents fail forward and teach their children to do the same? Here are some tips:

1. Acknowledge and accept failure: don't try to hide your failures or pretend they didn't happen. Acknowledge them and accept them as a natural part of the learning process.
2. Analyze and learn from failure: take the time to analyze what went wrong and what you can do differently next time. Use failure as an opportunity to learn and grow.
3. Model resilience and perseverance: show your children that you're not giving up when things get

tough! Model resilience and perseverance, and encourage your children to do the same.

4. Encourage risk-taking: encourage your children to take risks and try new things, even if they might fail. Help them understand that failure is not something to be afraid of, but rather, an opportunity to learn and grow.

5. Celebrate effort, not just success: finally, remember to celebrate effort, not just success. Help your children understand that hard work and perseverance are just as important as achieving their goals and praise them for their efforts, for example, "Wow, you tried so hard!"

Chapter 5

Identify

Identifying the *root cause* of your lack of confidence can be a powerful first step towards building greater self-assurance. For many people, it's difficult to pinpoint exactly what's holding them back. It might be a past failure, negative self-talk, or a deep-seated fear of judgment or rejection. But without addressing these underlying issues, it's hard to break out of the cycle of self-doubt.

For example, imagine you're someone who struggles with public speaking. You may assume that you're simply not cut out for it and that you'll never feel comfortable in front of a crowd. But if you take the time to reflect on *why you feel this way*, you may uncover deeper insecurities that are at play. Perhaps you were criticized for a presentation in the past, or you worry about being judged by your peers. By acknowledging and addressing these underlying fears, you can begin to build more confidence and take steps to improve your public speaking skills. You may also realize that hey, those fears were understandable when I was perhaps a child or awkward teen when I didn't quite know myself, but I know

I Feel Like a Giant!

myself now, and so I don't need to feel the same way as I did back then.

Another example might be someone who struggles with body image issues. They may have internalized negative messages about their appearance from family members, friends, or the media. By recognizing that these messages are not a reflection of their true worth and that they are no longer relevant, they can begin to challenge them and build a more positive self-image.

It's important to remember that identifying the root causes of our lack of confidence is not a one-time fix. It's an ongoing process of self-reflection and self-awareness. But with practice, we can develop a greater understanding of ourselves and the sources of our insecurities. From there, we can begin to take steps to address those issues and build greater confidence in ourselves, and hopefully let go of what is holding us back.

One of my struggles as a child was with reading and writing. I was a slow learner and would often make mistakes in front of my classmates. It was embarrassing and disheartening! But I knew I had to keep trying.

My newly adopted parents and the rest of my family were incredibly patient with me. They spent countless hours teaching me how to read and write. Although it drove them crazy at times, they never gave up on me. They knew the

Identify

importance of helping me build my confidence, especially since I was watching their every move.

In school, I started raising my hand more often, trying to participate and get the words and sentences correct. It was scary at first, but each time I got it right, it gave me a little bit more confidence to try again next time. I didn't want to be held back by my fear of making mistakes.

I am 5 foot 3 and a half inches tall, which was obviously too short to accomplish my basketball dream!. I was not Muggsy Bogues, the shortest NBA player; I was Ryan Stream, the guy who got cut, and I had to accept that I needed to do something else, to have a new dream.

From that moment on, after getting cut from the basketball team, I decided to join the military, and I knew that I had to work out and be extremely fit. I also wanted to have a white smile, be funny, be successful, and do all the things that would make me feel good.

I remember when I was 19 years old, I would read books on how to pick up girls! It's a true story, although at the time, I thought I was funny and pretty good-looking, I was a little insecure. So, I would read books and try to learn how to dance, yes, it's true! I was in the military, and I thought I would try to be the man that every woman would want to be with. I would focus so much on that stuff. Even growing up, my dad would yell, "Get out of the mirror! If you focused on other things besides your looks, you would do well." The truth

I Feel Like a Giant!

is, I was just insecure, and I learned that if I just did my best at marriage, family, work, and social life, and earned my sleep every night, I would be happy. And I am serious about my comment, "Earn your sleep." Every night, I put my head on my pillow, and I asked myself, "Did I earn my sleep, today?"

I may have already told this story, but some of the best advice I got one day was from my wife. I was feeling a little insecure. I was moping around the house with a bad attitude and just being all-around unpleasant to be around. My wife had enough and said, "If you are insecure, you need to work harder." I was mad she said it, and it hurt my feelings, but then I asked myself, "Am I doing the best I can?" I had been slacking off in my exercises, had been drinking soda and eating candy almost every day, and I was not a fan of the job I was working at. No wonder I was unhappy. Although I travel as a public speaker, I also work three days in the coal mining industry. I know what you're possibly thinking! Why the heck do you work there? The answer is, I am still trying to make my goals and dreams a reality. Most of us still need to keep our day job in order to do so! And in fact, it is very wise to keep that day job while pursuing other dreams.

Around the time COVID hit, I was getting booked seven times a month, and I had crushed my monthly coal mine income. I was on fire, but when COVID set in, I went to zero shows, and the economy shut down. It was tough. But I was very blessed to be working in a coal mine - I still had a job, unlike so many others.

Identify

But working in a coal mine is very hard work. Maybe during this chat with Elizabeth, I was just tired of working my weekend shifts, driving 76 miles one way, and then working for a 13.5-hour shift, then turning around and driving back home. It's a weekend job and allows me to have four days off during the week. So yes, it's tough but it's definitely a blessing, especially while I finished my associate's degree. (I got an associate's degree from Utah Valley University, and it was very, very hard for me, but I proved I could do it.)

Anyway, back to my wife giving me the best advice ever. The truth is, I am a busy person, but sometimes, actually many times, I slack off. I get complacent in my job, businesses, work, etc. I am a motivational speaker, and I want to practice exactly what I preach, not just be a man who reads a book and teaches it! I need to be a success story. At the same time, I am only human, and so are you. We are allowed to take a rest and recharge.

Elizabeth:

Growing up, I also struggled with confidence because I didn't think I was pretty. Everywhere I looked, I saw images of girls who looked nothing like me - perfect hair, flawless skin, and a perfect body. I would often wish I could look just like them, but I felt like I could never measure up.

My lack of confidence spilled over into my relationships, particularly with boys. I would let them walk all over me because I thought that dating them was the best I could do. I

I Feel Like a Giant!

didn't want to be alone, so I clung to them, even if they didn't treat me well.

However, as I got older, I realized that I needed to identify what was making me feel insecure in order to become more confident. I started taking care of myself by working out, eating healthily, and focusing on my skin. These small changes made me feel better about myself, both physically and mentally.

I also pursued my passion for esthetics and became a master esthetician. But first and most importantly, my husband and I started our family, and they are number one and will always be. Secondly, we started my business doing teeth whitening, buying and selling horses after they were trained, modeling, influencer work on social media, and investing in real estate and businesses. It was a way to prove to myself that I could accomplish something and be successful.

But the most important thing for me was being a role model for my daughters. I wanted them to see the importance of having confidence and identifying what made them feel a certain way. I also acknowledged that I was not always confident and sometimes needed a little motivational talk from my husband or friend to just listen to me and my feelings.

I believe that you don't have to be perfect or an amazing warrior, just turn to the direction you want to go in and start! And if you get lost along the way, just remember it can feel

Identify

good to be lost and heading in the wrong direction. These moments can be a time for reflection or sometimes, we even discover something new about ourselves or a new direction after getting a little lost. Whatever happens, I remain strong for myself and my family. I want my daughters to know that it's okay to have insecurities, you need to love yourself for who you are but you can always work on bettering yourself, and that it's important to work through any issues and come out stronger on the other side. They see me laugh, cry, pray, fall down, and stand up without hiding anything from them.

So, while my journey to confidence wasn't easy, (and is still always being worked on) it was worth it. Identifying what was holding me back allowed me to make changes that not only improved my own life but also allowed me to be a positive influence on others. It's important to remember that confidence is something you always have to work on, because life is about growing and learning, and if you're too comfortable, that might mean you're not trying hard enough.

Growing up, I was a huge fan of professional wrestling, and one of my idols was Dwayne "The Rock" Johnson. Every time he stepped into the ring, he would captivate the audience with his electrifying presence and trademark catchphrase, "Can you smell what The Rock is cooking?"

Back then, I didn't have many distractions or devices like we do now, so watching wrestling was a big part of my childhood. The Rock was the ultimate hero to me, the WWF

I Feel Like a Giant!

champion that no one could beat! He was built like a modern-day Hercules, and I couldn't help but admire his strength and confidence.

It wasn't until years later that I learned about the struggles The Rock had gone through in his life. As a teenager, his family went through some tough times and was evicted from their home. He had to move around a lot and attend multiple schools, which made it difficult for him to make friends and feel like he belonged. He also struggled with his body image and felt insecure about his looks, which affected his confidence.

Despite these challenges, The Rock remained determined to pursue his passions. He focused on football and eventually earned a scholarship to play at the University of Miami. After a brief stint in professional football, he transitioned to professional wrestling and quickly became one of the biggest stars in the industry.

However, even with his success, we can see that The Rock still struggled with his insecurities. He felt like he was "walking on eggshells" and constantly worried about failing. It wasn't until he sought help from a therapist that he was able to confront his issues and learn to embrace his flaws.

Today, The Rock is not only one of the biggest names in professional wrestling, but he has also become a highly successful actor in Hollywood. He is known for his confidence and charisma both on and off-screen, and he has

Identify

used his platform to speak openly about mental health and the importance of seeking help when needed.

The story of The Rock shows that even our childhood heroes need to identify their insecurities and struggles and work through them in order to be successful. It's important to remember that everyone faces challenges in life, and seeking help is a sign of strength, not weakness, just like The Rock. If he didn't seek help, I wonder where he would be now? The Rock's story is one that many people can relate to and draw inspiration from, and it reminds us that with determination and a willingness to confront our fears, we can overcome even the toughest obstacles!

Steps to Self-Identify

How can we all do a better job at learning how to identify what we need?

I like to use two analogies. Think about how as soon as you see your phone battery blinking or go into the red zone, about to shut off and die, you do whatever you can to plug your phone in, correct? Or what about when you get a text message or a phone call, what do you do? We answer the phone call and we answer the text. We text back the reply and solve the problem or answer the question from whoever was on the other line!

It's the same with our bodies. If I am angry or feeling a certain way, rather than leaving it off the charger til it shuts down!) I

I Feel Like a Giant!

will ask myself, "Okay, I am getting a message from my body, what is it trying to tell me?" Then I try to troubleshoot myself. How has my sleep been? Have I been exercising? Have I kissed my lover and told her I love her? Am I eating enough healthy foods, and drinking enough water? Am I stressed about something? What is bothering me? After I go down the list of things I start crossing them off. If they don't go away and if I can't identify the issue and solve it after going through the list, writing my feelings down or talking to my spouse, I will call and ask a therapist and see if I can make an appointment. There is nothing wrong or unmanly about talking about your feelings or hard times with a friend, especially a doctor or specialist who helps solve many other people's problems. What is wrong is letting these problems get worse by avoiding them.

I know this works from experience. In the book "Conquering Your Colosseum," you will read about my life in more depth, including growing up, drugs, adoption, and twice going to Afghanistan and fighting during a war. The part I would like to focus on, here, is struggling with PTSD.

What I'm about to share with you in this book, I had no idea about years ago. I didn't know this because I didn't even try to help myself by searching on the internet for what I was going through. I didn't have time for podcasts, and I didn't want to take the time to read a book. I did make time to fight with my wife, drink, and make foolish choices that were only crippling my marriage and mental health. I finally got the help I needed,

Identify

and now I'm back on track to working through things and being happier. But I still struggle with PTSD, especially after I hear a sound, see something, or just anything really that reminds me of Afghanistan.

My most current PTSD moment was when I was asleep and heard a helicopter fly over my house. I woke up ready for battle. My heart was pounding, and I just went right back to waking up in Afghanistan with gunfire and explosions going off around me. I then did exactly what I told you above, where I took a moment to identify the situation which helped me to identify where I was and what I was doing. I gave myself a self-evaluation (it didn't take long at all, but had such a powerful effect) and realized I was, in fact, asleep in my bed, my doors were locked, I was safe, I was by my wife's side, and everything was okay. I am okay. I tossed and turned, said a prayer, and then carried on.

You and I are not like phones that are immediately recharged without thought. So when we feel like our batteries are low or if something triggers us, we need to start to identify it, and then dissect the problem. It's actually pretty easy, and even more so once you get in the habit of it.

In psychological terms, a trigger is something that sets off an emotional response in someone due to past experiences or trauma. It can be a word, a sound, a smell, or any other type of stimulus that brings up memories and feelings associated with a past event.

I Feel Like a Giant!

When someone is triggered, they may experience intense emotions such as fear, anxiety, anger, or sadness. These emotions can be overwhelming and may cause them to act in ways that they wouldn't normally behave. It's important to recognize when you are triggered and to take steps to manage your emotions in a healthy way.

For example, if someone has a past experience with bullying and they hear someone else being bullied, it may trigger feelings of fear and anxiety. They may feel like they are back in that same situation and may react strongly to try and protect themselves or the person being bullied. Their reaction may or may not be appropriate for the situation.

Overall, being triggered is a natural and normal response to past trauma or experiences, but it's important to learn how to manage these emotions in a healthy way to avoid further harm.

Identifying our problems and getting help is a proactive choice that we can make for our own well-being, and in fact, the well-being of those around us. Sometimes we may blame others when we are triggered when in fact, even though it is very difficult, we must take responsibility for our own reactions. And if we have reacted more in relation to our trigger than that person's behavior we need to recognize that and may also take steps to apologize for our reaction. Dealing with our triggers involves taking responsibility for our own mental and emotional health and recognizing when we need support.

Identify

The first step is to become aware of what we're feeling and why we're feeling it. We can do this by asking ourselves questions and reflecting on our thoughts and behaviors. For example, if we're feeling anxious, we might ask ourselves, "What is causing me to feel anxious? Have I been taking care of myself? Have I been avoiding any important tasks or responsibilities?"

Once we've identified the problem, we can then take action to address it. This might involve seeking professional help from a therapist or counselor, talking to a trusted friend or family member, or engaging in self-care activities such as exercise, meditation, or journaling. It might even mean focusing on some work or a priority that you have been procrastinating with.

It's important to remember that seeking help is not a sign of weakness, but rather a sign of strength and self-awareness. By identifying our problems and taking steps to address them, we can improve our mental and emotional well-being and lead a more fulfilling life.

In summary, identifying our problems and getting help is a choice that we can make to take control of our own mental and emotional health. It involves becoming aware of our thoughts and feelings, taking responsibility for our own well-being, and taking action to address our problems.

Chapter 6

Dedication

Dedication and discipline are closely related concepts, but they represent different aspects of achieving a goal. Dedication is the initial driving force that propels a person towards a goal. It is the feeling of being committed to the goal, of being passionate about it, and of being willing to do whatever it takes to achieve it.

However, as the pursuit of the goal progresses, and as the initial enthusiasm can wear off, dedication begins to transform into discipline. Discipline is the ability to stick to a plan, to work consistently and methodically towards the goal, and to resist distractions and temptations. While dedication provides the initial spark, discipline is what keeps the flame burning over the long term.

The transition from dedication to discipline is important because it represents a shift from an emotional state to a more practical, pragmatic one. Dedication can be fleeting, and it can be influenced by external factors such as motivation or inspiration. Discipline, on the other hand, is a habit that can be cultivated and sustained over time.

Dedication

The process of transitioning from dedication to discipline can be challenging, but there are several steps that can help make it easier.

1. Set a clear goal: the first step is to identify a specific, measurable, and realistic goal. This goal should be something that is meaningful to you and that aligns with your values and interests. It should also be something that you can realistically achieve with hard work and dedication.

2. Develop a plan: once you have identified your goal, you need to develop a plan to achieve it. This plan should include specific actions that you can take on a daily or weekly basis to move closer to your goal. It should also include timelines and deadlines to keep you on track.

3. Start small: when you are first starting out, it is important to start small and build momentum. This means setting achievable goals and taking small steps towards your larger goal. This will help you develop a sense of accomplishment and build confidence, which will help you stay motivated over the long term.

4. Hold yourself accountable: discipline requires self-accountability. This means being honest with yourself about your progress, and holding yourself to a high standard of performance. You can do this by tracking your progress, setting deadlines, and rewarding yourself for achieving milestones.

5. Be flexible: finally, it is important to be flexible and adaptable. Life is unpredictable, and sometimes

unexpected challenges or opportunities arise. Being able to adjust your plan and your mindset to accommodate these changes is key to staying dedicated and disciplined over the long term.

When I think of someone who has dedication and discipline I first think of the military <u>special forces and elites</u>. The men and women who join the special forces and elite military groups are some of the most disciplined individuals in the world. Their training is grueling, both physically and mentally, and only a small percentage of those who attempt it actually make it through.

From the moment they begin their training, these individuals are subjected to intense physical demands. They may be required to run miles in full gear, climb ropes and obstacles, carry heavy loads for long distances, and perform a wide range of other physically demanding tasks. These grueling exercises are designed to push them beyond their limits and test their mental toughness as well as their physical stamina.

But it's not just about physical strength. The most elite military groups require a very high level of mental discipline that is unmatched in any other profession. They must be able to stay calm under intense pressure, remain focused on their mission despite distractions and obstacles, and work together as a team in the face of adversity.

In order to achieve this level of discipline, special forces trainees are subjected to a variety of mental and emotional

Dedication

stressors. They may be deprived of sleep, subjected to extreme temperatures, forced to operate under simulated combat conditions, and even placed in isolation for extended periods of time. Through it all, they are expected to maintain their composure and focus on their mission.

But perhaps the most important aspect of the discipline required to become a member of the special forces is the ability to push past the limits of pain and discomfort. These individuals must be willing to endure physical and mental suffering beyond what most people can even imagine. They must learn to embrace discomfort as a necessary part of their training and accept it as a natural part of their job.

In the end, the discipline required to become a member of the special forces is not just about physical strength or mental toughness. It's about the willingness to sacrifice, to put the needs of the team above one's own personal comfort, and to embrace the challenges and hardships that come with the job. It's about having the courage to face one's fears and the determination to never give up, no matter how difficult the task may seem. And it's about having the mental and physical fortitude to carry out their mission, no matter what.

When I think of dedication and discipline, I think of Mike Tyson, the former heavyweight boxing champion, who is known for his incredible dedication and discipline in the sport of boxing. Tyson grew up in a rough neighborhood in

I Feel Like a Giant!

Brooklyn, New York, and he turned to boxing as a way to channel his energy and stay out of trouble.

Tyson's dedication to boxing was evident from an early age. He started training when he was just 13 years old and quickly developed a reputation as a fierce fighter! Tyson's training regimen was grueling and intense, but he never wavered in his commitment to the sport.

One of the most famous stories about Tyson's dedication and discipline involves his daily routine of doing sit-ups until he felt his butt burn! Tyson would reportedly do hundreds of sit-ups every day, pushing himself to the limit and beyond. He was so committed to this routine that he would often walk around with his arms crossed over his chest, like the great warriors of the past.

Tyson's dedication to boxing paid off in a big way. He became the youngest heavyweight champion in history at the age of 20, and he went on to win 50 of his 58 professional fights. Tyson's speed, power, and ferocity in the ring were unmatched, and he became one of the most dominant boxers of his era.

While Tyson's career was not without controversy, his dedication and discipline in the sport of boxing are undeniable. He was willing to do whatever it took to succeed, and his commitment to his craft inspired many other fighters and athletes to follow in his footsteps. Tyson's legacy as a

Dedication

boxing legend is secure, and his dedication and discipline are a big part of what made him so great.

Michael Jordan is widely regarded as one of the greatest basketball players of all time, and his success on the court can be attributed in large part to his incredible discipline and work ethic. Jordan's dedication to his craft was legendary, and he would often put in hours of extra work before and after team practices, as well as during the offseason.

One of the most famous examples of Jordan's discipline and work ethic comes from his early years with the Chicago Bulls. In his book "Relentless: From Good to Great to Unstoppable," Jordan's former trainer Tim Grover describes how Jordan would often arrive at the Bulls' practice facility at 5:00 AM to work on his shooting and conditioning before the rest of the team even showed up. Jordan would then go through a full team practice, and then stay after to work on his game even more. Talk about putting in the hours!

Jordan's discipline also extended to his diet and nutrition. He was known for being very strict about what he ate and drank, and would avoid alcohol and junk food in order to maintain his peak physical condition. In addition, Jordan was known for getting plenty of rest and taking care of his body, often getting massages and treatments to help prevent injuries.

But Jordan's discipline wasn't just limited to his physical preparation. He was also incredibly disciplined when it came to his mental approach to the game. Jordan was known for his intense focus and mental toughness, and would often visualize himself making game-winning shots and making key plays in his mind before they even happened on the court. He also had a very competitive nature and was always looking for ways to improve his game and gain an edge over his opponents.

Overall, Jordan's dedication and discipline were key factors in his success on the basketball court, and his approach to the game continues to inspire athletes and non-athletes alike to strive for greatness in all areas of their lives.

Similarly, top business leaders have a high level of dedication and discipline. Take Jeff Bezos the founder of Amazon, who is known for his unwavering dedication and discipline in his pursuit of success. He was born in Albuquerque, New Mexico in 1964 and was raised by his mother and stepfather. As a child, Bezos had a passion for technology and entrepreneurship.

In 1994, Bezos founded Amazon.com, an online bookstore that would eventually become the largest online retailer in the world! Bezos was dedicated to his vision of creating a company that offered a wide selection of products and exceptional customer service. He worked tirelessly to build Amazon from the ground up, putting in long hours and pushing himself to the limits.

One of the ways in which Bezos demonstrated his discipline and dedication was through his willingness to take risks. He

Dedication

left his well-paying job at a Wall Street firm to pursue his dream of starting Amazon. He also invested heavily in the company during its early days, despite the fact that it was not yet profitable.

Bezos also prioritized his health and well-being, recognizing that physical and mental discipline was essential for achieving his goals. He was known to maintain a strict exercise routine and diet, and he would often start his day with a workout. In interviews, he has actually credited his dedication to his health as a major factor in his success.

Additionally, Bezos was disciplined in his approach to innovation and experimentation. He was willing to try new things and make mistakes, recognizing that failure was a necessary part of the learning process. This approach helped Amazon to become one of the most innovative and successful companies in the world.

In summary, Jeff Bezos is an example of the discipline and dedication required to achieve great success. His willingness to take risks, prioritize his health, and innovate helped him to build one of the most successful companies in history.

Elon Musk is another example of a highly disciplined and dedicated individual. He is known for his work as an entrepreneur, inventor, and engineer. Musk has founded multiple successful companies, including SpaceX, Tesla, Neuralink, and The Boring Company.

I Feel Like a Giant!

One of the keys to Musk's success is his unwavering dedication to his goals. He has a clear vision of what he wants to achieve, and he works tirelessly to make that vision a reality. He is known for his incredible work ethic, often working 80-100 hours per week!

In addition to his dedication to his work, Musk is also highly disciplined in his personal life. He follows a strict daily routine, which includes waking up at 5 am, exercising, and reading for several hours each day. He also practices meditation and spends time with his family.

Musk's discipline and dedication have been crucial to his success. He has overcome numerous challenges and setbacks in his career, but he has never given up on his goals. His ability to stay focused and committed has allowed him to achieve incredible things, including sending rockets to space, creating innovative electric cars, and developing technology that could change the future of humanity!

In short, Elon Musk is a great example of how discipline and dedication can lead to incredible success. His commitment to his work and personal life has helped him achieve his goals and make a significant impact on the world.

All of these individuals are known for their unwavering dedication to their companies and vision.

Dedication can also be found in everyday individuals who are committed to their personal or professional growth, such as

Dedication

students who study diligently to achieve their academic goals, parents who work hard to provide for their families, or volunteers who devote their time and energy to serving their communities.

Ultimately, dedication is not limited to a particular person or profession but can be demonstrated by anyone who sets a goal, works tirelessly towards it, and refuses to give up until they have achieved it. Absolutely any of us can find success with dedication and discipline.

In conclusion, dedication and discipline are both essential components of achieving a goal. While dedication provides the initial drive, discipline is what sustains the effort over the long term. By setting clear goals, developing a plan, starting small, holding yourself accountable, and being flexible, you can transition from dedication to discipline and achieve the success you desire.

Chapter 7

Education

I hope you enjoyed hearing about all of those outstanding individuals in Chapter 6, (including everyday people who are just as dedicated and disciplined in areas in their lives). I really enjoyed writing about them! When I see stories about these multi-millionaires and billionaires it is so inspiring because it's not only unbelievable the impact they have in the world, but also the honing of their talents through their dedication and discipline. It wasn't just luck of having a talent and going off and enjoying that talent - they worked at it, so hard!

One other thing they all have in common is they are all educated. I would like to share with you a little about their education, and then talk about education in a little more depth.

For Jeff Bezos, education was a key factor in his success as the founder of Amazon. He received a degree in electrical engineering and computer science from Princeton University, which gave him the knowledge and skills necessary to create a technology-based business. Additionally, he has been known to have a passion for learning and constantly seeks out new information to help drive his business forward.

Education

<u>Elon Musk</u>, who is known for his groundbreaking work in the fields of space exploration and electric cars, also has a strong educational background. He holds degrees in both physics and economics and has even pursued graduate studies in applied physics and materials science at Stanford University. This education has given him the knowledge and skills to push the boundaries of technology and innovate in areas that were previously thought impossible.

In the case of <u>Michael Jordan</u>, his education was focused on basketball. He played college basketball at the University of North Carolina, where he honed his skills and developed a deep understanding of the game. He was always striving to learn more about the sport and how he could improve mentally and physically. This education, combined with his dedication and discipline, led him to become one of the greatest basketball players of all time.

Special forces personnel, such as <u>Navy SEALs and Army Rangers,</u> also require a high level of education and training. They undergo rigorous physical and mental training, including specialized combat training, language courses, and cultural education. They must also continually educate themselves on new techniques and tactics to stay ahead of the ever-evolving threats they face. As you can see, the learning never stops.

As I'm writing I feel like I could push myself a little harder at getting some more of my goals crossed off the to-do list! They are so inspiring!

I Feel Like a Giant!

Education is an important factor in the success of individuals in various fields, from business to sports to special forces. It provides the knowledge and skills necessary to excel in their chosen area of expertise and helps them stay at the forefront of innovation and progress. However, it is also important to note that, regardless of one's educational background you can still succeed.

For many years, obtaining a college degree has been regarded as the most important qualification for landing a good job and having a successful career. But with the advent of new technologies and the emergence of various online resources, it has become increasingly clear that a college degree is not the only path to success. There are so many things we can actually learn online - the online resources alone are just mind boggling and many people have started to turn to alternative sources of education, such as YouTube, podcasts, online courses, and books, to learn new skills and gain knowledge. In this section, we will explore why education is all around us, and why a college degree may not be necessary for success.

So we're going to go further into recognizing that knowledge is not limited to formal education institutions such as universities and colleges. The internet has revolutionized the way we access and consume information, making it possible for anyone with an internet connection to learn new things from the comfort of their own homes.

Education

One of the biggest advantages of these alternative sources of education is their accessibility. Unlike traditional universities and colleges, online resources are often free or available at a low cost. This makes it possible for anyone, regardless of their financial background, to access valuable knowledge and skills. In addition, many of these resources are self-paced, allowing learners to study at their own speed and on their own schedule, making it possible to learn while juggling work or other commitments.

Another benefit of alternative sources of education is the flexibility they offer. Unlike traditional education institutions, online resources are not bound by schedules or geographic locations. Learners can access them from anywhere in the world, at any time, allowing for greater flexibility and convenience. And think of the time we can save without having to travel. Additionally, many online courses and educational platforms offer certifications and credentials that are recognized by employers, making them a credible and valuable addition to a resume.

While there are certainly benefits to obtaining a college degree, it is important to recognize that it is not the only path to success.

Many successful entrepreneurs, such as Mark Zuckerberg of Facebook, Richard Branson of Virgin Group, and Steve Jobs of Apple, dropped out of college to pursue their passions and build successful businesses. These individuals were able to gain the knowledge and skills they needed through other means, such as self-education, mentorship, and on-the-job experience.

In conclusion, the world we live in today offers us a vast array of educational resources that are easily accessible, flexible, and often more affordable than traditional education institutions. We are truly very, very lucky to have this knowledge at our fingertips. With the rise of online resources such as YouTube, podcasts, online courses, and e-books, it is clear that formal education is no longer the only path to success. It can help us understand the world around us. It can teach us about history, science, art, culture, and so much more. With a deeper understanding of the world, we can make more informed decisions and engage in conversations with others in a more meaningful way.

However, it is important to remember that education, whether it is obtained through formal institutions or alternative sources, is a lifelong journey that requires dedication, discipline, and a commitment to continuous learning.

Knowledge is indeed power, and it can provide us with the confidence we need to pursue our goals and aspirations..

Additionally, knowledge can make us more confident in ourselves and our abilities. When we learn new skills or gain new knowledge, we feel a sense of accomplishment and pride. This can help us build self-esteem and improve our mental health.

Furthermore, the pursuit of knowledge can also open doors to new opportunities. As we learn new things and develop new skills, we become more marketable and attractive to employers. We may even discover new passions and interests that lead us down unexpected and exciting career paths.

Ultimately, whether through a formal college education or alternative sources of learning, the acquisition of knowledge is a powerful tool for personal and professional growth. By continually seeking out opportunities to learn and expand our horizons, we can become more confident, capable, and successful in all aspects of our lives.

Chapter 8

Navigate

Before the invention of advanced navigation systems, people relied heavily on maps to navigate their way around. Maps are essentially a representation of the world on a flat piece of paper, and it takes a certain level of skill and knowledge to read and interpret them correctly.

In the past, travelers would carry maps with them and use them to navigate through unfamiliar territory. They would have to understand things like scale, orientation, and symbols on the map in order to accurately determine their location and direction of travel. It was a much more manual process and required a lot of mental effort and skill to be proficient. Even folding up the maps was a challenge!

However, maps were not always completely reliable. They could be outdated, incomplete, or even inaccurate in some cases. This could result in travelers getting lost or taking longer than expected to reach their destination.

With the advent of modern navigation systems, such as GPS and smartphone apps, navigation has become much simpler and more accurate. We can now enter an address or destination into our devices and they will provide us with turn-by-turn directions, estimated travel times, and even real-time traffic updates to help us avoid delays. It's amazing!

While modern navigation systems are certainly convenient, it is still important to understand how to read and interpret maps. They are a valuable tool for outdoor enthusiasts, hikers, and anyone who travels in areas where GPS or cellular signal may be unreliable. By understanding how to navigate with a map, we can be prepared for any situation and ensure that we always arrive at our destination safely and efficiently. I bet you are wondering where I am going with this? You thought this was a book about life skills, not map reading!

Well, just as we use a navigation system to find our way when driving, we also need to navigate our lives to achieve success and build confidence. In life, there are many roads to choose from, and it's up to us to determine the path that will lead us to where we want to go.

Navigating our lives requires self-awareness and a clear understanding of our goals and aspirations. Just like setting a destination in our GPS, we need to set goals for ourselves and have a clear vision of where we want to be in the future. This helps us to stay focused and motivated, even when we encounter obstacles along the way and prevents us from getting too lost. (A little bit lost is okay, as Elizabeth mentioned earlier, but too lost, is another story).

I Feel Like a Giant!

Just like driving, navigating our lives requires us to make decisions and take action. We can't just sit back and wait for things to happen. We need to be proactive and take control of our lives. This means making tough decisions, taking risks, and learning from our mistakes.

When we navigate our lives with purpose and direction, we develop a sense of confidence and self-assurance. We know where we're going, and we have a plan for how to get there. This helps us to stay focused and motivated, even in the face of adversity.

In conclusion, just as a navigation system helps us find our way when driving, we need to navigate our lives to achieve success and build confidence. By setting goals, making decisions, and taking action, we can create the life we want and develop a sense of purpose and direction.

Navigating through life can be a complex journey, and sometimes we may find ourselves straying from our intended path. However, it's important to remember that even when we get off course, these moments can serve as valuable learning opportunities. It's natural to experience setbacks or obstacles along the way, but the key is to keep pushing forward and trust the process.

There are times when we may encounter unexpected challenges or events that cause us to deviate from our plans. Just like a ship caught in a storm, we may be blown off course or even forced to change direction entirely. However, it's important to remember that even in these moments, we can still learn and grow. Perhaps this detour will lead us to discover new opportunities or perspectives that we may not have encountered otherwise.

Trusting the process means having faith in the journey, even when the destination is uncertain. It means believing in ourselves and our ability to navigate through whatever challenges come our way. While it's natural to feel anxious or uncertain at times, we can build confidence by focusing on our strengths and staying committed to our goals.

In the end, navigating through life requires both perseverance and adaptability. We must be willing to make adjustments and course-correct when necessary, while also staying true to our core values and beliefs. By doing so, we can cultivate the confidence and resilience needed to overcome obstacles and achieve success. The steps on dedication will also help with this chapter.

So, let's take control of our lives, set our destination, and navigate our way to success!.

Here are some steps to help with navigating your life:

1. Set clear goals: identify what you want to achieve and set specific and achievable goals. Write them down and break them down into smaller, manageable steps.
2. Plan and prioritize: make a plan and prioritize your goals. Decide which goals are the most important and

create a plan to achieve them. Make sure your plan is flexible and adaptable.

3. Take action: take action towards your goals! Start with small steps and build momentum. Don't be afraid to make mistakes or fail. Use those experiences as learning opportunities.

4. Evaluate your progress: regularly evaluate your progress and adjust your plan if necessary. Don't forget to celebrate your successes and learn from your failures.

5. Stay focused: stay focused on your goals and don't let distractions or setbacks derail you. Stay motivated and keep moving forward.

6. Seek support: always seek support from family, friends, or a mentor who can provide guidance and encouragement. Join a group or community of like-minded individuals who can support you on your journey.

Remember, navigating in life is not always easy, but with dedication, determination, and a clear plan, you can achieve your goals and become more confident and successful. Trust the process and believe in yourself.

A Story About Navigating

Elizabeth and I recently purchased an investment home in Provo, Utah. We were thrilled with the idea of making a profit and had what we believed was a solid plan in place. Unfortunately, our initial excitement quickly turned to frustration when we struggled to find contractors to work on the property. To make matters worse, one of the workers we hired didn't show up, leaving my wife and me to do most of the work ourselves. This was not part of the plan!

Eventually, we managed to complete the condo and found a single mother with three children to rent it. We were happy to provide her with a home, but things took an unexpected turn when we learned that she was not a legal resident and could be deported to Mexico along with her kids if she didn't have a place to live in the US.

Despite an offer that would have netted us a $100,000 profit, we decided not to evict the lady and her children.

A few months later, the sink in the apartment got plugged and her son left the water running, causing the upstairs to flood. The kids were downstairs asleep, and the older child woke up to water dripping from the ceiling and lights. To cut a long and pretty awful story short, we had to redo the entire apartment. Once again, I had to do most of the work alone because we didn't know many contractors and everyone was too busy in Utah. Our daughters were in school, and my wife was doing more than her part, managing their activities, school work, and helping me with meals and finances. It was not a fun time!

One day, I felt defeated. We had sold another house and didn't make any profits because the $25,000 profit went into this project in order to fix it. Our navigation map had promised a lot of money, but here I was, sitting on a bucket, asking God what He was trying to teach us. I was doing all I could, but I was tired and I was not a contractor. My wife was doing more than I could ask, while I was always away doing other things. Then, I teared up when I realized - God was teaching me how to build! I added new light fixtures, countertops, and walls, among lots of other things. After months of hard work, the condo was finally ready for the market once again. The profits we made from selling our property put us in a perfect position to invest in a better opportunity that was perfectly timed for this moment. God had a better plan for us, and sometimes we need to trust the process and keep working even if we feel lost.

Another important thing to remember is that as you pursue your goals, there will always be people who try to steer you off course or distract you from the path you're trying to take. However, it's essential to remain focused and determined, because your goals are important to you for a reason. Don't be deterred! Listen carefully to the advice of others, but also, trust your instincts and your goals if they feel right.

One of the main reasons why people struggle with confidence is due to fear. Specifically, there are three primary fears that can hold people back:

- Fear of failure
- Fear of success
- Fear of judgment from others.

These fears can be daunting and overwhelming, but it's essential to be heroic and confident in facing them head-on.

The fear of failure is a common one, as many people worry about what will happen if they don't succeed. But it's important to remember that failure is a natural part of the learning process, and it's often through failure that we learn and grow the most! Embracing the possibility of failure can actually help to build confidence and resilience.

The fear of success is less talked about, but it can be just as crippling as the fear of failure. Success can come with its own set of challenges, such as increased responsibility, expectations, and pressure. However, it's important to recognize that success is something to be celebrated and that you deserve to achieve your goals.

Finally, the fear of judgment from others is another common fear that can hold people back. It's natural to worry about what others might think or say about us, but it's important to remember that ultimately, the only person you need to answer to is yourself. It's crucial to stay true to your values and beliefs, even if it means going against the opinions of others.

In conclusion, it's important to stay focused on your goals and remain confident in the face of fear. By embracing the possibility of failure, celebrating success, and staying true to yourself, you can overcome these fears and achieve great things.

Chapter 9

Truth

Let's talk about truth. And what I mean about truth, is being honest with what you are trying to achieve, about how you are really going, being truthful about your struggles, about when you may need help and also, being truthful about your successes and celebrating them.

But firstly, lying can indeed damage our relationships and leave us feeling guilty and ashamed. Lying also hinders our ability to be truthful to ourselves and to others. It's important to understand that being truthful doesn't mean being perfect, but rather being honest about our mistakes, weaknesses, and struggles.

Setting goals can be a great way to improve our confidence and achieve success, but it's important to make them realistic and achievable. Instead of setting lofty goals that are difficult to attain, start with small, attainable steps and build up momentum from there.

It's also important to recognize that setbacks and failures are a natural part of the process, and it's okay to make mistakes as long as we learn from them and keep moving forward. By staying dedicated and committed to our goals, we can overcome obstacles and achieve the success and confidence we desire. We must also learn to embrace failure and see it as an opportunity to learn and grow. By viewing setbacks as valuable learning experiences, we can develop the resilience and confidence we need to keep pushing forward even when the going gets tough.

In addition to setting goals and being truthful to ourselves, taking care of our physical health through good nutrition and exercise can also boost our confidence and well-being. By treating our bodies with care and respect, we can feel better both physically and mentally.

Finally, being kind to ourselves and talking to ourselves positively can also help improve our confidence. Instead of focusing on our flaws and mistakes, we should celebrate our strengths and accomplishments and treat ourselves with compassion and understanding.

By being truthful to ourselves, setting realistic goals, staying dedicated, taking care of our physical health, and being kind to ourselves, we can improve our confidence and achieve the success we desire. By talking to yourself positively and focusing on your abilities, you can overcome challenges and achieve your goals.

"It will not be easy"

I Feel Like a Giant!

"Nothing worth sacrificing will be easy" - a simple phrase that holds within it a powerful truth. To achieve great things in life, we must be willing to put in the hard work, to make sacrifices and face challenges that test our limits. Remember, it's never too late to start making positive changes in our lives, about being honest about where we are at and where we are heading, and every small step counts towards a more confident and fulfilling future.

It's important to acknowledge that failure is a natural part of the learning process. Don't be afraid to take risks and learn from your mistakes. By identifying what makes you feel less confident, you can work on improving those areas and become more self-assured.

But it's not just about the effort we put in - it's also about our mindset. To succeed, we must be confident in ourselves and our abilities. We must believe that we are capable of overcoming any obstacle that stands in our way.

Confidence is not something that comes easily to everyone, but it can be developed and strengthened over time. It starts with recognizing our strengths and weaknesses and then working to improve ourselves in areas where we may be lacking.

Ultimately, being confident means believing in ourselves and our ability to achieve the things we want in life, even when the path ahead is difficult. We can be like David, we can feel like giants! So remember, nothing worth sacrificing will be

Truth

easy, but with confidence and perseverance, we can overcome any obstacle and achieve greatness.

Thank you for spending your precious moments with us throughout these pages! We hope these stories and steps have helped you on your journey towards building confidence and that you too, can feel like a giant as you start ticking off those achievements!

emember to thank those who have helped you along the way, including God. May He continue to guide and bless you as you navigate through life. We hope to see you all down the road. God Bless.

-Ryan and Elizabeth Stream

www.ingramcontent.com/pod-product-compliance
Lightning Source LLC
Chambersburg PA
CBHW050517100526
44581CB00001B/5